CREATED BY
WENDY AND CURTIS MAYS

YOUR MONEY 101
WORKBOOK

7 STEPS TO BUILDING WEALTH AND DUMPING DEBT EVEN WHEN STARTING FROM SCRATCH

FI UNIVERSITY
A HOUSE OF FI PUBLICATION

7 STEPS TO BUILDING WEALTH AND DUMPING DEBT EVEN WHEN STARTING FROM SCRATCH

TABLE OF CONTENTS

5 **OVERVIEW OF COURSE**
THE SEVEN LESSONS

6 **WELCOME**
A WORD FROM WENDY AND CURTIS

26 **LESSON 1**
KNOW WHERE YOU WANT TO BE

37 **LESSON 2**
Know Where You Are

52 **LESSON 3**
Determine Your Net Worth

64 **LESSON 4**
The Bones of Your Budget

76 **LESSON 5**
Refining Your Money Master Plan

TABLE OF CONTENTS

76 **LESSON 6**
Implementation

91 **LESSON 7**
Next Steps

92 **RESOURCES**
Extra Journal Pages and Printable Trackers

Time Grows What is Planted
- Unknown

"Money is only a tool. It will take you wherever you wish, but it will not replace you as the driver."

— Ayn Rand

YOUR MONEY 101

This workbook is for you if you are sick and tired of your current financial situation and ready to do the work to change your financial trajectory.

IT'S TIME TO GET TO WORK...

Seven Steps to Building Wealth and Dumping Debt - Even When You Are Starting From Scratch

- ❏ Lesson 1: Know where you want to be. What do you want your financial future to look like?
- ❏ Lesson 2: Know where you are.
- ❏ Lesson 3: Determine your net worth.
- ❏ Lesson 4: The bones of your budget.
- ❏ Lesson 5: Refining your budget.
- ❏ Lesson 6: Implementation.
- ❏ Lesson 7: Next Steps.

WELCOME FROM WENDY AND CURTIS

DECIDING TO SAVE MONEY AND BE DEBT FREE – ONCE AND FOR ALL WAS THE BEST DECISION WE EVER MADE.

Maybe some of this sounds familiar to you…

Before deciding to become **FINANCIALLY INDEPENDENT** we were:

- Carrying almost $1,000,000.00 in debt
- Drowning with six-figure student loan debt
- Living pay-check to pay-check
- Making really good money – but had nothing to show for it
- Close to ZERO in retirement saved
- No way to help our children attend college
- AFRAID of our financial future and the legacy we were going to leave our children

Then, just like you have today, we made the life-changing decision. We were going to re-write the ending of our story. We would become FINANCIALLY INDEPENDENT before we turned 55 and leave a legacy for our kids!

Let me tell you a little more about Curtis and I. We are Gen-Xer's in our late forties. Married over 23 years and we have six children. Our family of four exploded to a family of 8 several years ago when we decided to trust God and say yes to a plan we never envisioned for ourselves.

Our boys are our WHY. And it is because of them that we have mercilessly tackled our goal to become Financially Independent. Below is what we have been able to accomplish so far:

- Our overall debt has been reduced by about **$650,000.00**!

- We now live on one income for the first time in our lives. I am able to stay home to be more available to the special needs in our family. Something we **NEVER** thought possible.

- I was able to retire my law practice in late 2018.

- We increased our savings rate to 29% (from about 5-7%).

- We reduced our monthly expenses by **$9,931.00**.

- We began real estate investing and will see a positive cash flow of approximately $1100.00 a month from real estate investments.
- We are **consumer debt free** – all that remains are our student loans.

But, our goal here today is to not talk about us. It is to help **YOU**.

We want to help you become Financially Independent.

To be **DEBT FREE**.
To **SAVE MORE**.
To **SPEND LESS**.
and to **INCREASE YOUR INCOME**, so that you can live **LARGE** on less.

We want you to live joyful and full lives – not burdened by the worry of money. We want you to find the same HOPE that we found just a few years ago.

Working through YOUR MONEY 101 - is the first step to creating the generational wealth you desire for your family.

WE ARE GLAD YOU ARE HERE!

LESSON 1 - KNOW WHERE YOU WANT TO BE

Nothing becomes a life change until you assign the highest value to it. - Wayne Cordeiro

TASK 1: UNDERSTANDING YOUR WHY

Use the following pages to think about what you want your life to look like in the next 5, 10, 20, 50…years.

What would your finances look like?

Would you be debt free?

Would you have a fully funded retirement plan?

Are you living in your dream home?

Are you retired?

Focus on how these make you FEEL.

BE SPECIFIC…. "In five years I WILL….."

End of Lesson 1

Building Your Money Foundation
Finding Your WHY

FIND A QUIET SPOT AND ANSWER THESE FOUR QUESTIONS:

Q1: THINK ABOUT HOW YOU WANT YOUR LIFE TO LOOK IN (5/10/15/20) YEARS. IN ORDER TO ACCOMPLISH THIS, WHAT WOULD BE DIFFERENT ABOUT YOUR CURRENT FINANCIAL CIRCUMSTANCES? WHAT DOES THIS LOOK LIKE?

Q2: NOW, WORK YOUR GOAL BACKWARDS AND LETS QUANTIFY WHAT YOU NEED TO ACCOMPLISH WITH YOUR FINANCES TO ACHIEVE THAT GOAL?

Q3: WHAT ARE THE BIGGEST BARRIERS TO YOU ACCOMPLISHING THE FINANCIAL GOALS YOU LISTED IN QUESTION 2? WHAT ARE THE AREAS THAT WE CAN ASSIST YOU THE MOST WITH?

Q4: FINALLY, YOU WILL NEED TO LOOK OVER YOUR LAST THREE MONTHS OF BANK STATEMENTS. EXAMINE THE 3 HIGHEST AREAS OF SPENDING. YOU CAN DO THIS MANUALLY OR CHOOSE FROM VARIOUS APPS/SOFTWARE TO DO THIS AUTOMATICALLY (MINT, PERSONALCAPITAL, QUICKBOOKS...)

HOW WELL DO THESE AREAS OF SPENDING SUPPORT YOUR ANSWERS TO QUESTIONS 1-3?

I am in control of my finances

LESSON 2: KNOW WHERE YOU ARE

You can't begin to plan your future, unless you first know where you are. This part of your journey is going to be HARD. Likely emotional - but worth it.

REMEMBER - YOU CAN DO HARD THINGS.

1. Review three months of bank statements and credit card statements and track where your money is going. You can do this in a few different ways.

    a. Upload in to Intuit, Personal Capital or Mint. (You may have to go back in and manually correct categories to make sure that they are attributed correctly. For instance, the purchase at the gas station was "food" and not "fuel".)

a. An Excel or Google Spreadsheet.

b. The old fashioned way - pen and paper.

2. Write down your totals for each category. We will be coming back to this later.

End of Lesson 2

TAKE A BREATH! YOU DID AWESOME. THIS WAS HARD - CELEBRATE....

...FRUGALLY - LIKE A $5 PIZZA OR SOMETHING....AND PAY WITH CASH.

LESSON 3 - DETERMINE YOUR NET WORTH

Time Grows What is Planted. - Unknown

Just like building a home, when it comes to managing your money, you have to start from the ground up. We know that a solid foundation is absolutely critical to long term success. Building your foundation is essentially establishing your baseline from which you will move forward towards your ultimate goal (your Why).

To begin this process, you first have to determine your current Net Worth.

Using the FINDING YOUR NET WORTH worksheet, you will be organizing your current assets and your current debts into the appropriate categories. The difference between these two totals represents your current Net Worth.

After you have completed the worksheet, use the the following blank journal feelings to catalogue your thoughts.

Are you surprised? Pleased or disappointed?

Finding Your Net Worth

YOUR NET WORTH IS YOUR ASSETS MINUS YOUR LIABILITIES

YOUR ASSETS

YOUR LIABILITES

YOUR NET WORTH

I live in abundance

Finding Your Net Worth

YOUR NET WORTH IS YOUR ASSETS MINUS YOUR LIABILITIES

YOUR ASSETS
What do you have that is of value?

Home
Paid-off Car
Bank Accounts
Investments
Other Accounts

YOUR LIABILITES
What do you owe?

Mortgage
Car Loans
Credit Cards
Personal Loans
Student Loans

YOUR NET WORTH

Subtract the Total Liabilities from Your Total Assets.

If you sold everything of value and then paid off all of your debts, the amount left over would be your net worth.

I live in abundance

HOW ARE YOU FEELING? TAKE A BREATH YOU ARE DOING GOOD WORK! ADULTING IS HARD AND WE CAN'T MAKE BIG GAINS, WITHOUT DOING THE HARD WORK.

BE PROUD OF YOURSELF FOR TAKING CHARGE OF YOUR FINANCIAL FUTURE.

End of Lesson 3

LESSON 4 - THE BONES OF YOUR BUDGET

He Who Has a Why Can Endure Any How - Frederick Nietzsche

It's Budget Day!

Don't dread your budget...if that work makes you anxious - call it a Spending Plan. This is where you tell your money what to do.

When your money is working with you instead of against you, it's much more fun to play with!

Fill out your MONEY MASTER PLAN

(****you can print as many of these as you need)

End of Lesson 4

MONEY MASTER PLAN

WHAT'S LEFT?

Income	
Expenses	
Left Over Income	

YOUR FOUR WALLS

EXPENSE	AMOUNT
Mortgage/Rent	
Second Mortgage	
HOA Dues	
Home maintenance	
Taxes if not paid through impounds	
Insurance	
Electric	
Water and Sewer	
Telephone	
Trash	
Gas	
Other	
Other	
Other	
Other	
Other	
Other	
Other	
Other	
TOTAL HOUSING	
PERCENTAGE OF INCOME	

ALL DEBT

EXPENSE	AMOUNT
Student Loan #1	
Student Loan #2	
Credit Card #1	
Credit Card #2	
Credit Card #3	
Credit Card #4	
Other	
Other	
Other	
TOTAL DEBT	
PERCENTAGE OF INCOME	

TRANSPORTATION EXPENSES

EXPENSE	AMOUNT
Auto Loan Payment	
Insurance	
Public Transport	
Fuel	
Other	
Other	
Other	
TOTAL TRANSPORTATION	
PERCENTAGE OF INCOME	

INCOME

INCOME	AMOUNT
Net Payday	
Net Payday	
Self Employment	
Other	
Other	
Other	
Total income	

TRANSFERS INTO SAVINGS

SAVINGS	AMOUNT
Retirement	
Emergency Fund	
College Funds	
After-Tax Investments	
Other	
Other	
Other	
Other	
TOTAL SAVINGS	
PERCENTAGE OF INCOME	

LIVING EXPENSES

EXPENSES	AMOUNT
Groceries	
Dining Out	
Entertainment	
Pet Expenses	
Clothes & Grooming	
Cell phone	
Internet	
Cable	
Child-care	
Education/Tuition	
Child support/alimony	
Health & Fitness	
Charity	
Life Insurance	
Health Insurance	
Disability Insurance	
Long-term care Insurance	
Other	
Other	
Other	
Other	
Other	
Other	
Other	
Other	
TOTAL LIVING EXPENSES	
PERCENTAGE OF INCOME	

TOTAL EXPENSES

TOTAL SPENT	AMOUNT

LESSON 5 - REFINING YOUR MONEY MASTER PLAN

No one improves by accident. - John Maxwell

Now it's time to go back and look through your budget data, and start identifying places where you can begin making cuts to your budget!

Take a moment to review the recommended guidelines.

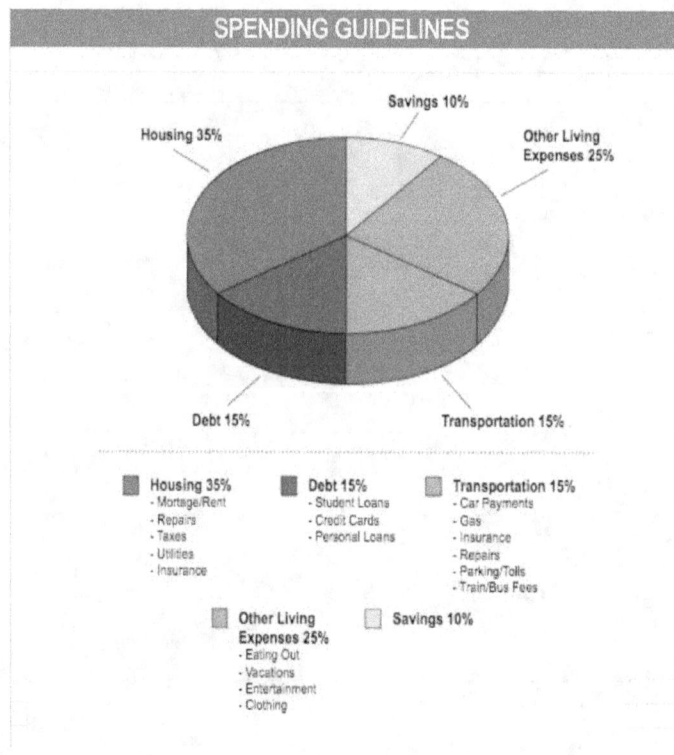

Are there areas that you are overspending?

Areas that you are able to cut completely - even just temporarily?

Look at every spending category and ask the question:

- Can I reduce this expense?
- Can I cut this expanse entirely?

Please sketch out a minimum of 3 possible areas that you feel you can adjust your budget.

Some ideas to get you started:

- Meal prep and plan.
- Limit dining out.
- Cut transportation costs.
- Cut housing costs.
- Limit extra-curriculars.
- Cut cable.
- Lower energy expenses.
- Get a roommate.
- Now your turn!
- Use the following pages to further brainstorm.

LESSON 6 - IMPLEMENTATION

The BEST way to predict your future is to create it. - Abraham Lincoln

YOU HAVE MADE DEEP BUDGET CUTS, NOW WHAT?

Now that you have made the difficult phone calls, cancelled and reduced services, made the hard decision of asking if you can move into your parent's basement for six months to cut your housing expenses (only joking - unless this really is an option for you....)

Now what do you do with all that money you have created in your budget?

IN ORDER OF PRIORITY:

1. Emergency Fund - at least $1000.00
2. Pay Off All Consumer Debt*
3. If you have a 401k that matches, contribute enough to get the match
4. Fully Funded Emergency Fund (3-6 months of living expenses)**
5. Max Out All Retirement Accounts
6. Pay Off Mortgage or Fund After Tax Accounts (pay off remaining student loans)

*If you have large amounts of student loans, you will pay the minimum on these until after you have completed Step 5 (Fully funded retirement accounts).

**If you are self-employed, We recommend a much larger stash of cash in your emergency fund. At least 6 months to a year.

YOUR BEGINNING EMERGENCY FUND

In the beginning, you just want enough in an emergency fund to take care of unexpected happenings, like a car repair or some other TRUE emergency. Date night or Christmas is not an emergency and should be saved up for - and not by raiding your savings.

THE TWO METHODS TO PAYING OFF DEBT

With most of the extra money you have found in your budget you are going to begin attacking your debt. There are two methods and you can choose whichever one makes the most sense to you.

>The Snowball Method - Begin with the debt with the smallest balance and throw all of your extra money at it until it is paid off. All the while you are paying the minimums on everything else. Once the first debt is paid off, you take the amount you were paying on that item, plus the extra money you have made in your budget and begin attacking the next highest balance, and so on and so on.

>The Avalanche Method - This method is identical to the first, except you begin with the account with the highest interest rate.

GET THAT MATCH!!!

If you have a 401K or other retirement account where your employer matches your contributions, this is a 100% return on your money right out of the gate, so don't waste it. Get that match!

FULLY FUNDED EMERGENCY FUND

Once you have paid off your consumer debt and have taken advantage of your employer match, your next task is to save enough to provide for yourself in the event of a big emergency, like a job layoff or illness. Typically, it is recommended that you have three to six months of expenses saved. However, my suggestion is that if you are self-employed that you increase this to six-twelve months.

MAX OUT ALL RETIREMENT ACCOUNTS

You are on the home stretch! Now you are going to be kicking things into high gear and really start planning for your future.

Saving for your retirement is HUGE! Let the power of compound interest work FOR YOU. The earlier you get to this step the better. But don't fret if you feel behind the ball here. The best time to start - IS NOW!

In addition to saving for your 65-year old self, you are likely reducing your current tax-liability now. BONUS. *(Not advice - Be sure to speak with your own tax professional.)*

PAY OFF YOUR MORTGAGE or INVEST IN AFTER TAX ACCOUNTS

You have made it! The last step is to pay off your mortgage or take the rest of your extra money and invest in after-tax investment accounts. Which one you choose, depends on what matters most to you. There are benefits to both….and if you are able to do both at the same time?

GO FOR IT!

(If you have large student loans, you will be paying off them in this step as well.)

Check the back of this workbook for trackers you can use to help meet your goals

End of Lesson 6

LESSON 7 - NEXT STEPS

This marks the end of YOUR MONEY 101 - 7 Steps to Building Wealth and Dumping Debt - Even When Starting From Scratch

Even though you have done a lot of hard work, the process of gaining control of your money has just begun.

REMEMBER You have to keep working and adjusting your plan. Your budget is fluid. You can and should change it if you need to.

In fact, it will take you a few months of tweaking to get it just right. This is just a matter of timing and is to be expected.

Your Final Assignment...

Be patient, remember your WHY. Revisit and stretch your goals, and stay on track.

And finally....YOU CAN DO THIS. YOU ARE IN CONTROL OF YOUR FUTURE.

Continue to find ways to SAVE MORE, SPEND LESS AND INCREASE YOUR INCOME!

Love and Prosperity, Wendy and Curtis

RESOURCES

VISIT OUR WEBSITE: https://houseoffi.com/

Listen to our podcast and YouTube Channel for inspiration, and know that we are on this journey with you. You can find us on our website as well as one iTunes, Apple Podcast, GooglePlay, Spotify and most other platforms.

If you need additional support, you can find us as Facebook, Instagram, Pinterest and Twitter.

AT THE END OF THIS WORKOOK ARE TRACKERS TO CHART YOUR PROGRESS AS YOU ACCOMPLISH EACH TASK.

Mortgage Payoff Tracker

Current Balance

Years Left on Mortgage

New Target Date

I will pay off my mortgage in ____ years.

I will accomplish this by paying $____ extra in principle ever year.

Mortgage Payoff Tracker

YEAR _____   Goal:

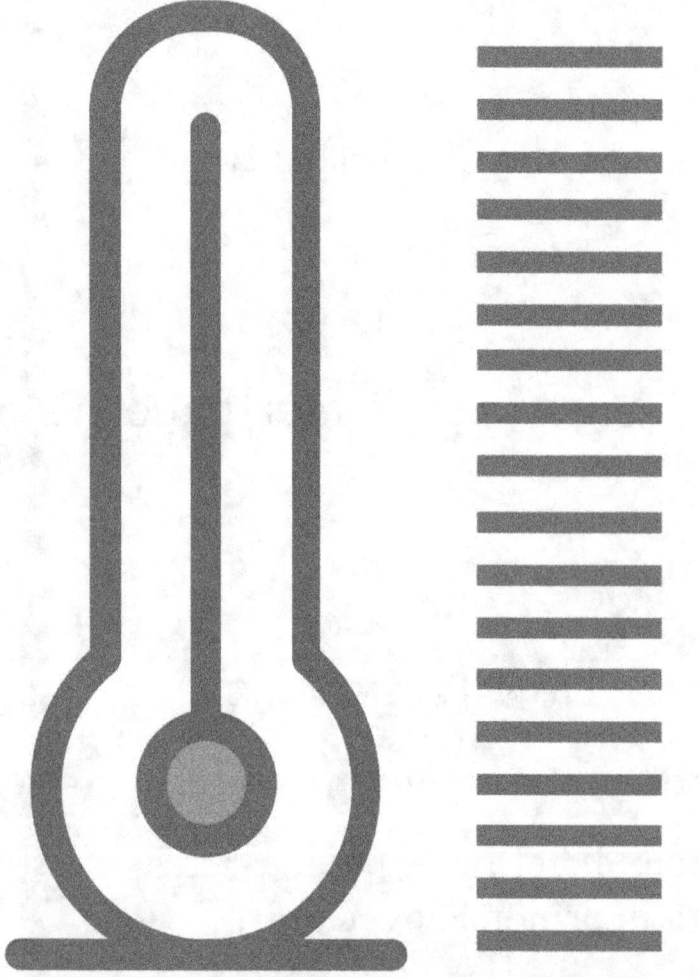

Debt Payoff Tracker

 Current Balance of All Debt

 Target Date to DEBT FREEDOM

I will be DEBT FREE
(not including my mortgage)
in ___ years.

I will accomplish this by paying an extra $___ to my overall balance every year.

I am the master of my wealth.

Debt Payoff Tracker

YEAR _____   Goal:

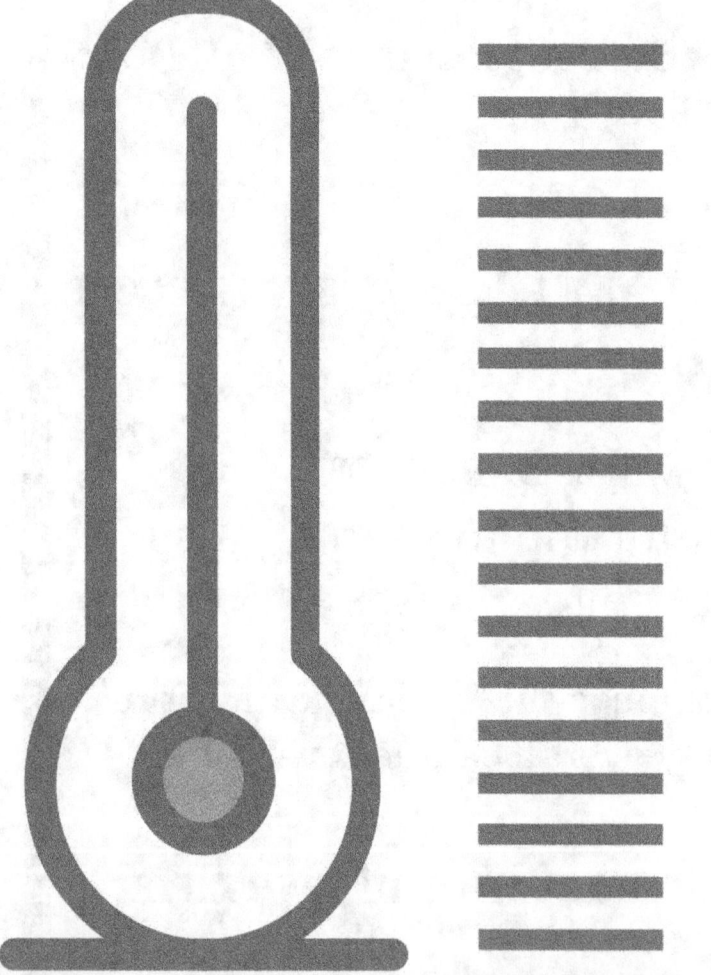

Debt Payoff Tracker

List of Debts

Debt	Current Balance	Date Paid Off

I am open and receptive to all the wealth life offers me.

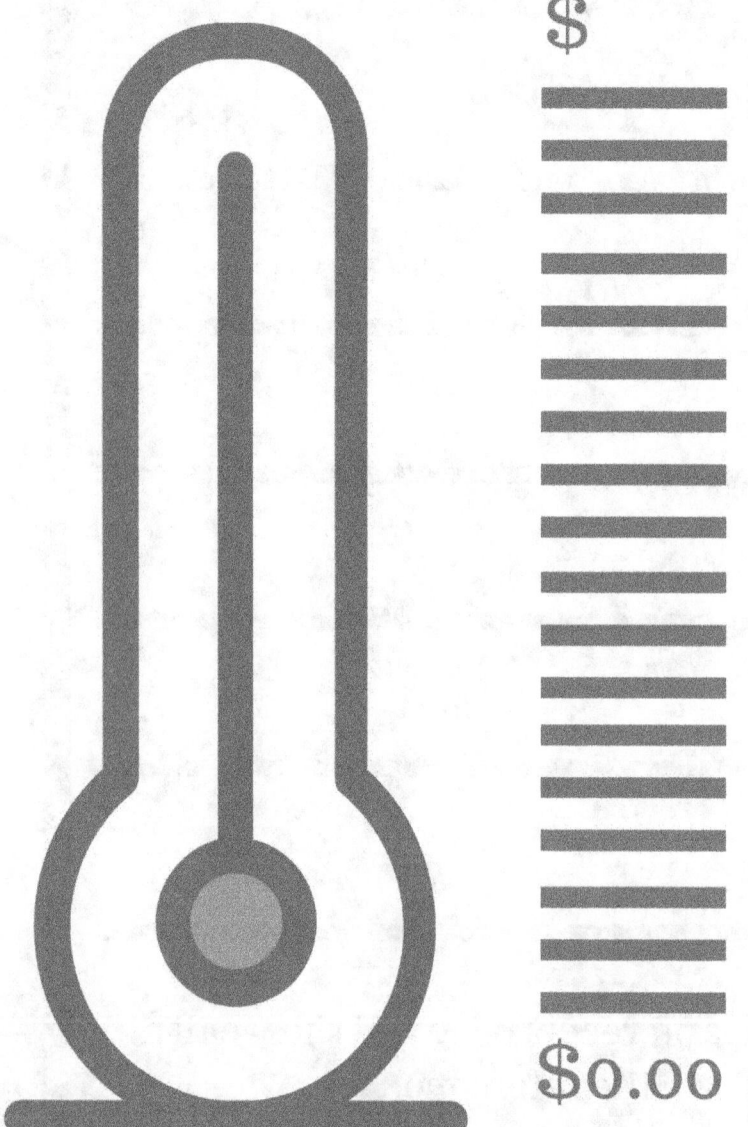

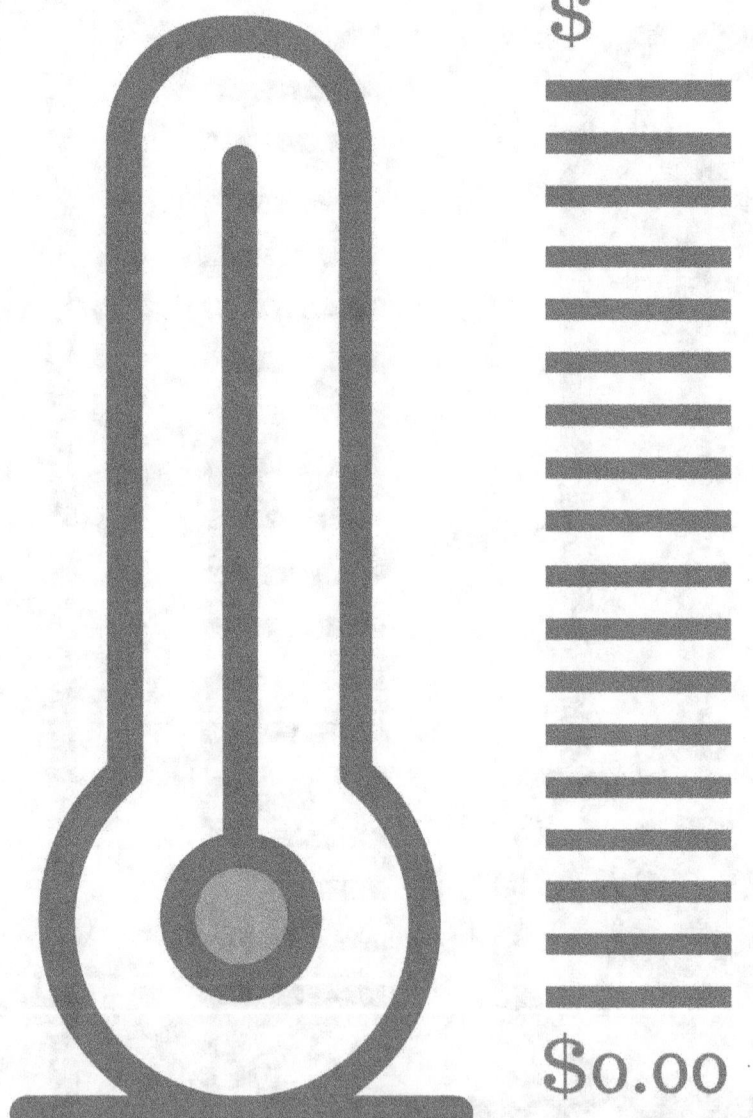

www.ingramcontent.com/pod-product-compliance
Lightning Source LLC
Chambersburg PA
CBHW080547220526
45466CB00010B/3061